I0786612

THIS IS YOUR DAY,
DAUGHTER!

Start at the X to reach the
puppy. Then color the pictures.

X

Connect the dots and color
your birthday guest!

The sheep sends birthday wishes to the most darling DAUGHTER in the world!

Start at the X to complete the maze. Then color your birthday balloons.

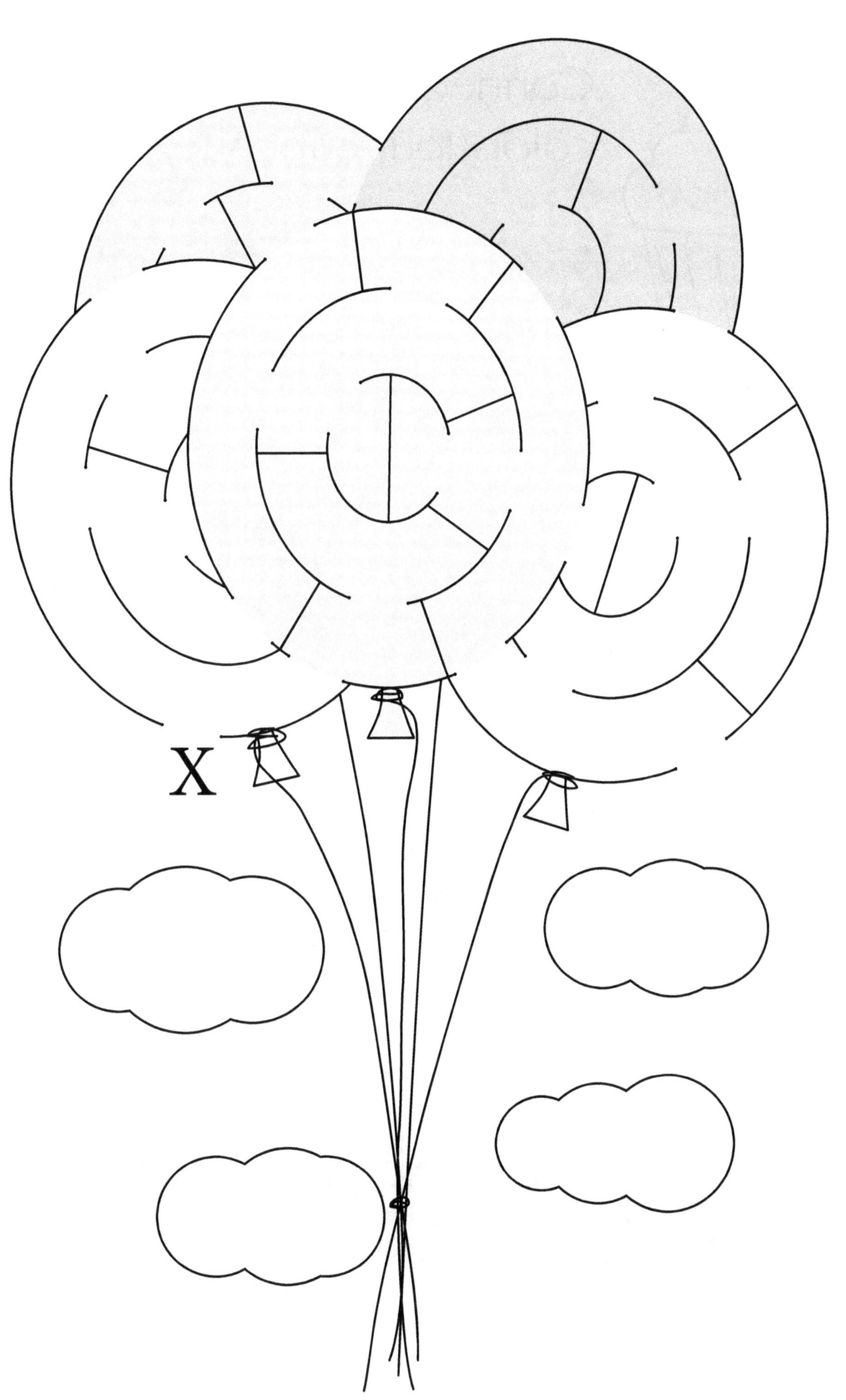

X

Connect the dots and
color your cupcake.

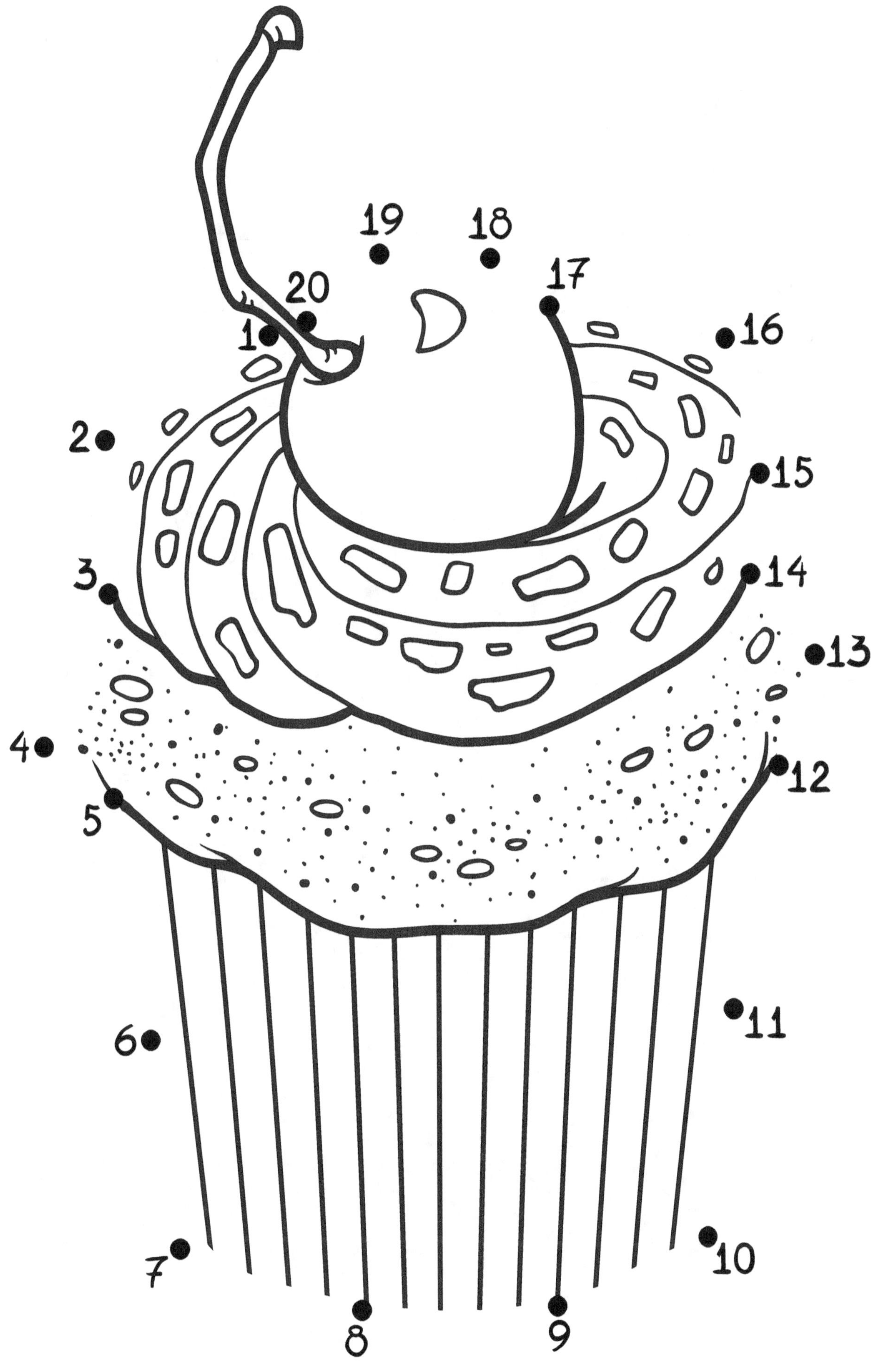

Count the number of candles, cherries, and strawberries on the cake.
Bonus: What's the total number of decorations on the cake?

_ _ _ _ _

HOW MANY?

Color, cut, and glue the cake
on another sheet of paper.
What is your favorite flavor?

CUT & GLUE
COLOR
1
CUT OUT
2
GLUE
3
USE EXAMPLE OR YOUR IMAGINATION

Color the party reindeer!
The reindeer wants to
join the celebration with
my amazing DAUGHTER!

HAPPY
BIRTHDAY

Start at the X to help the kitten reach the cupcake.

X

How many diamonds, hearts, and circles do you see on the cupcake?

Bonus: What is the total number of decorations? _____

HOW MANY ?

Start at the X to complete the maze. Then color your party hat!

X

Color the ice cream cone.
Then cut and glue the
ice cream cone on a blank
sheet of paper.
What is your favorite flavor of
ice cream? __________________

CUT & GLUE
COLOR
1
CUT OUT
2
GLUE
3
USE EXAMPLE OR YOUR IMAGINATION

Color the hippopotamus.
The hippopotamus is sending
warm birthday wishes to
my DAUGHTER on her
special day!

HAPPY
BIRTHDAY

Connect the dots and
color your birthday present.

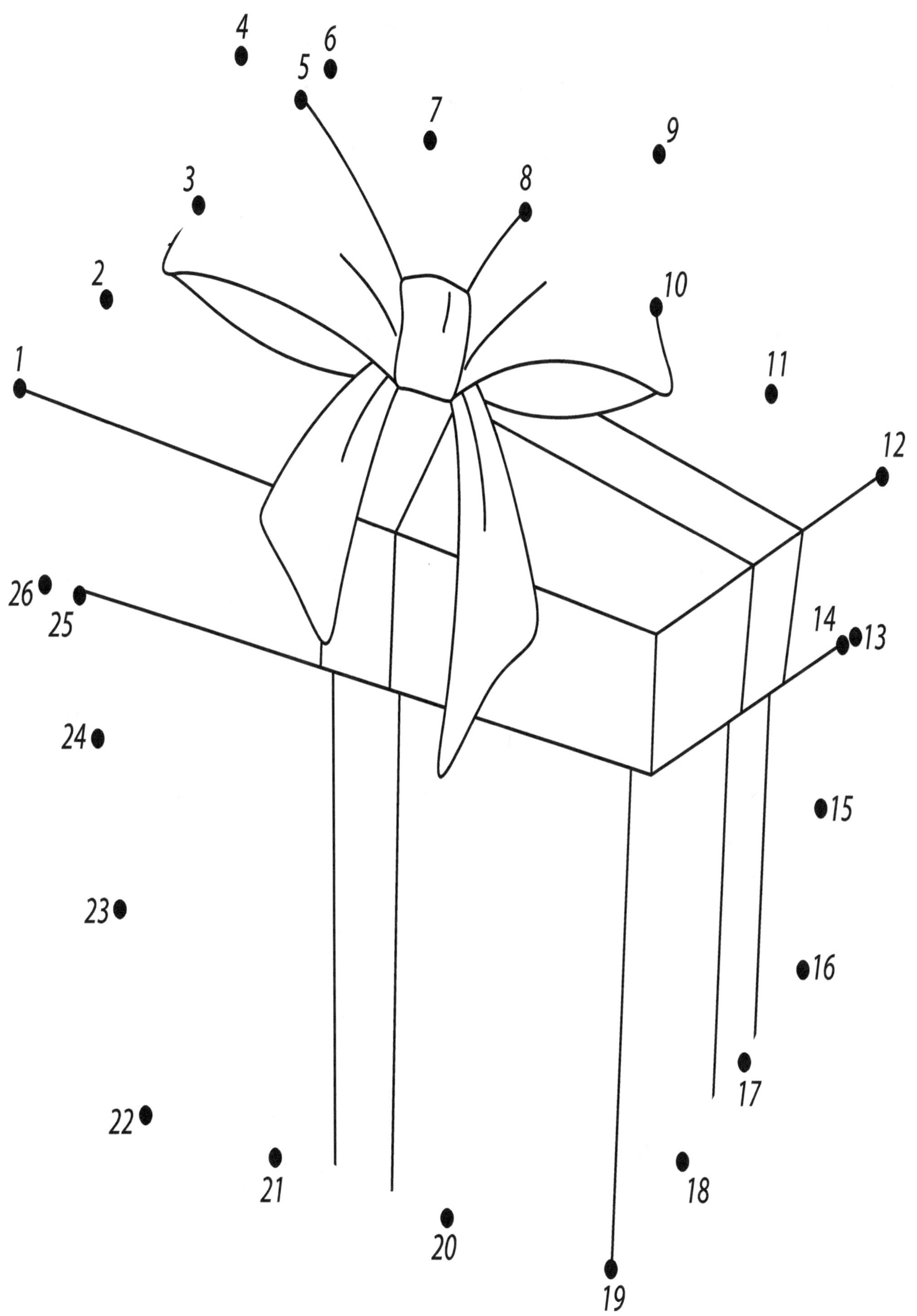

4
6
5
3
2
7
9
8
1
10
11
12
26
25
14
13
24
15
23
16
22
17
21
18
20
19

Follow the maze lines from the puppy to the cake. Then color the pictures.

Happy
Birthday

Color, cut, and glue the cupcake on another sheet of paper.

CUT & GLUE
COLOR
CUT OUT
GLUE
USE EXAMPLE OR YOUR IMAGINATION
1
2
3

Which maze should the bear follow? Find the correct maze and then color the pictures.

Start at the X to complete the
maze. Then color the cupcake.
Do you want a cupcake
or cake for your birthday?

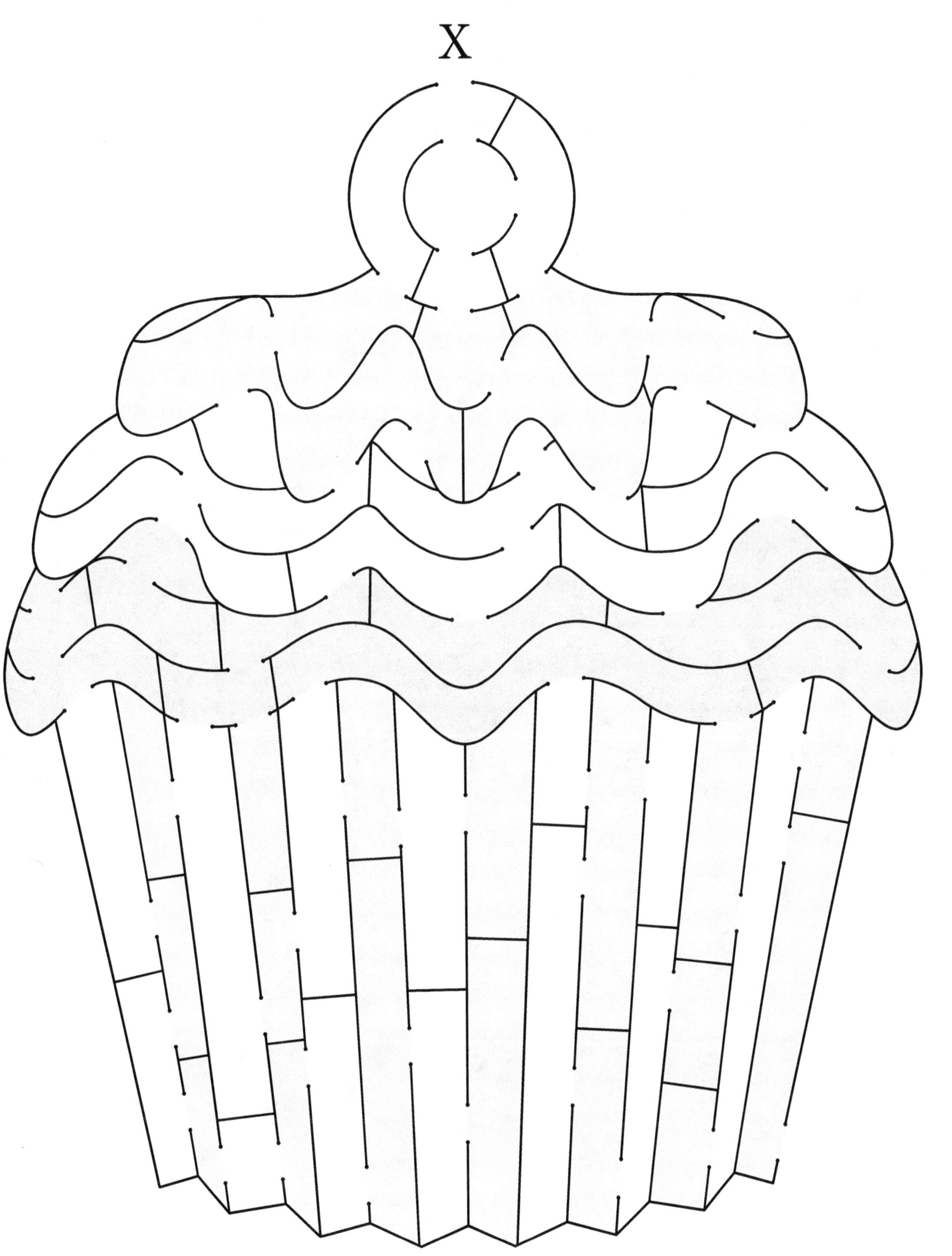
X

Start at the X to help the clown at the top reach the juggling clown at the bottom.

X

Connect the dots and
color the delicious cake!

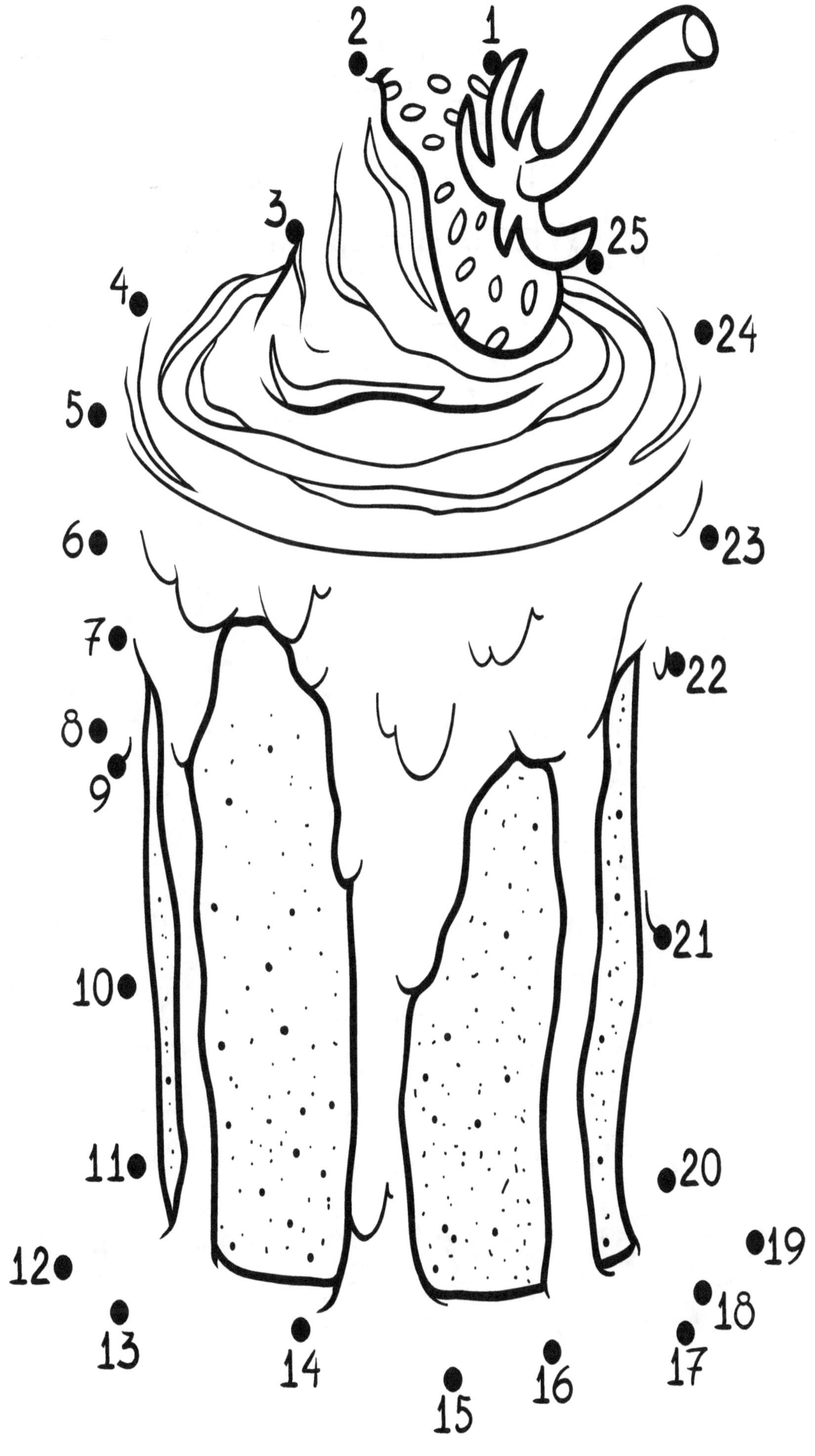

Draw your birthday bow on the grid. Then color the bow with your favorite color(s)! What are your favorite colors?

Copy and color the picture of the bow!

Color, cut, and glue your birthday clown on another sheet of paper.

CUT & GLUE
COLOR
1
CUT OUT
2
GLUE
3
USE EXAMPLE OR YOUR IMAGINATION

Start at the X to complete the maze. Then color your birthday cake! Do you need to add more candles?

DAUGHTER, don't forget to make a wish before you blow out your candles!!

Color the puppy and your party decorations! The puppy loves birthday gifts, too!

DAUGHTER, can you use the arrows to help the unicorns reach each other?

Connect the dots and color your birthday bow! How about adding polka dots or stripes to decorate your bow?

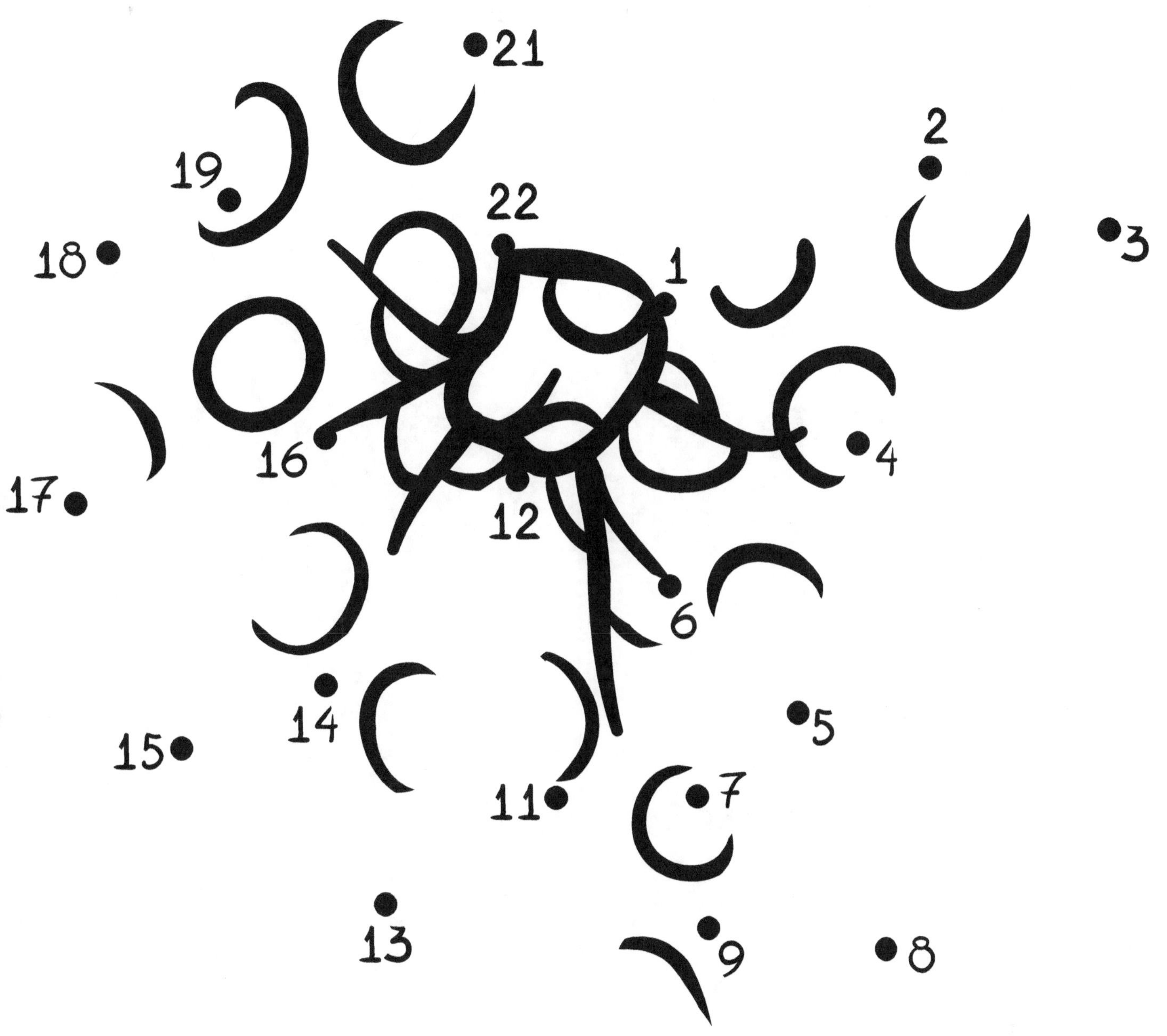

THIS ACTIVITY BOOK IS DEDICATED TO MY DAUGHTER ON HER BIRTHDAY!

HAPPY
BIRTHDAY

HAPPY BIRTHDAY DAUGHTER! FUN ACTIVITY BOOK:
Mazes, Coloring, Connect the Dots, Counting, & More!

Copyright 2018
By Florabella Publishing, LLC
florabellapublishing@yahoo.com
All rights reserved. No part of this book may be reproduced in any form or by any electronic means including information storage and retrieval systems, without permission in writing from the authors. The only exception is by a reviewer, who may quote short excerpts in a review.

www.ingramcontent.com/pod-product-compliance
Lightning Source LLC
Chambersburg PA
CBHW080043260726
48658CB00007B/2712